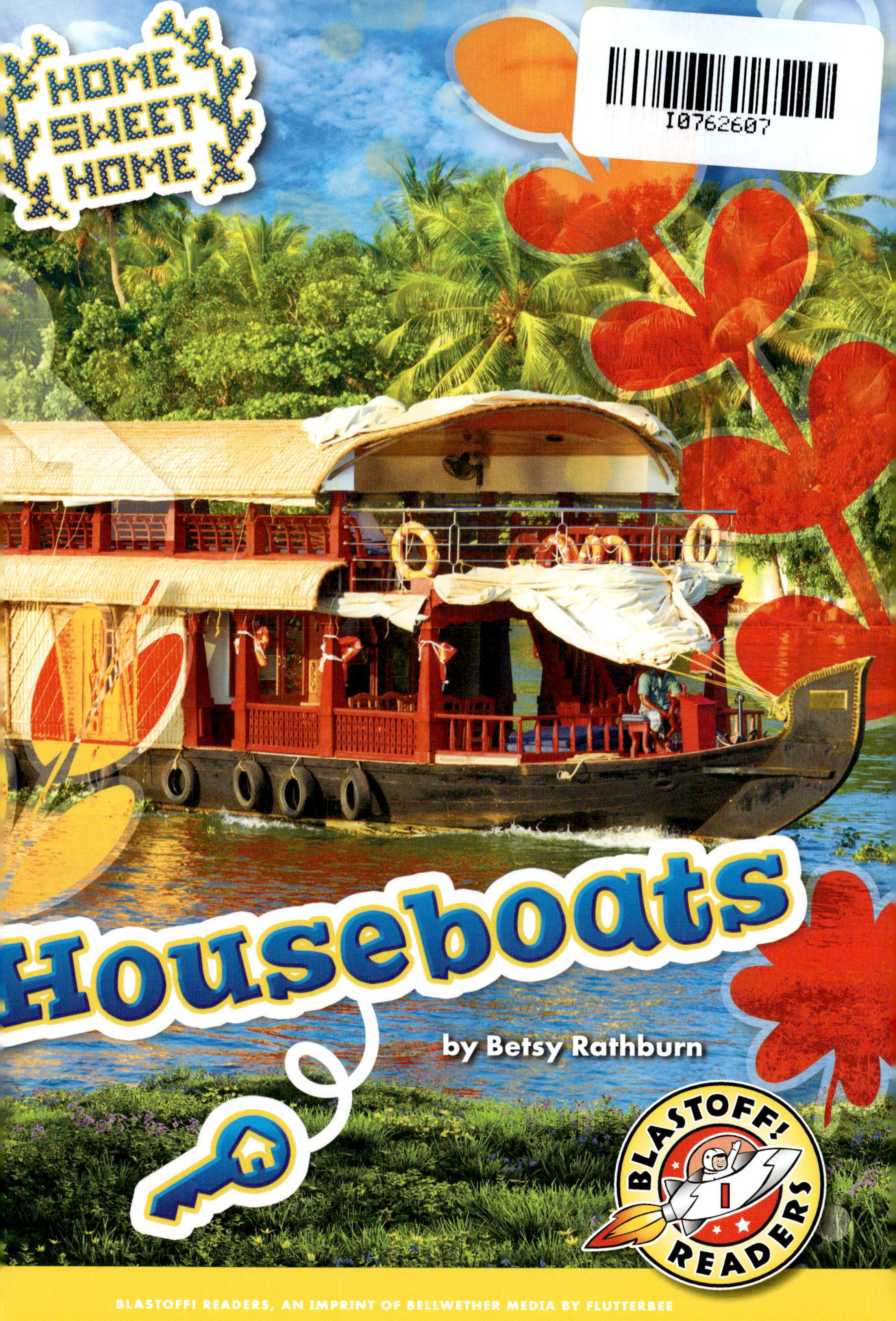

Houseboats

by Betsy Rathburn

BLASTOFF! READERS, AN IMPRINT OF BELLWETHER MEDIA BY FLUTTERBEE

Blastoff! Readers are carefully developed by literacy experts to build reading stamina and move students toward fluency by combining standards-based content with developmentally appropriate text.

Level 1 provides the most support through repetition of high-frequency words, light text, predictable sentence patterns, and strong visual support.

Level 2 offers early readers a bit more challenge through varied sentences, increased text load, and text-supportive special features.

Level 3 advances early-fluent readers toward fluency through increased text load, less reliance on photos, advancing concepts, longer sentences, and more complex special features.

★ **Blastoff! Universe**

Reading Level

Grade K

Grades 1–3

Grade 4

This edition first published in 2027 by Bellwether Media, Inc.

For information regarding permission, write to Bellwether Media, Inc., Attention: Permissions Department, 3500 American Blvd W, Suite 150, Bloomington, MN 55431.

Library of Congress Cataloging-in-Publication Data is available at www.loc.gov or upon request from the publisher.

ISBN: 9798898800277 (hardcover)
ISBN: 9798898802806 (paperback)
ISBN: 9798898801519 (ebook)

Editor: Rebecca Sabelko Designer: Andrea Schneider

Printed in the United States of America, North Mankato, MN.

Table of Contents

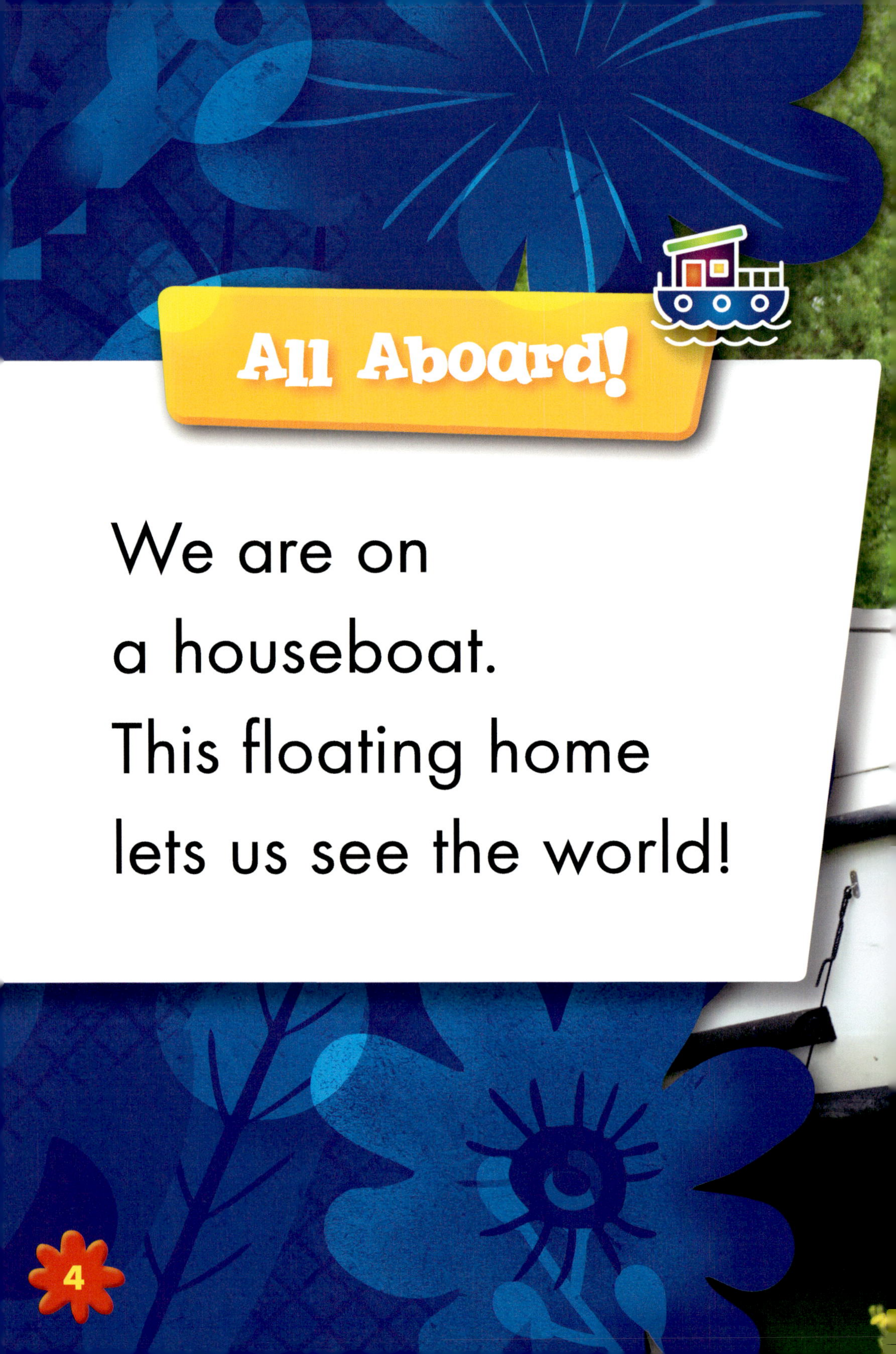

All Aboard!

We are on
a houseboat.
This floating home
lets us see the world!

What Is a Houseboat?

Houseboats are boats that people live in.

Some people live in houseboats in the summer. Others live in houseboats all year!

Size of a Houseboat
2 school buses
1 houseboat

People keep their houseboats in **marinas**. They park in **slips**.

slips
marina

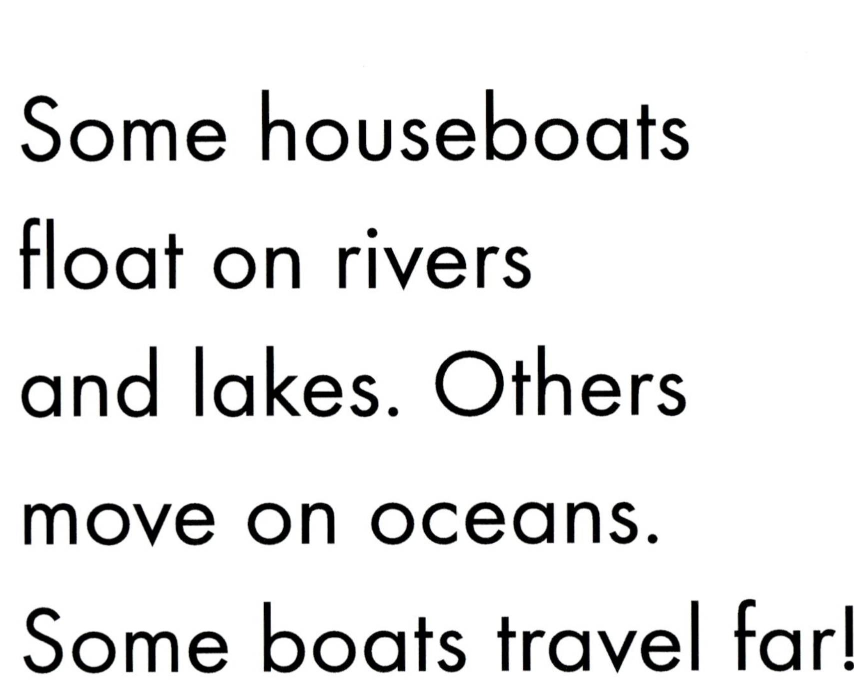

Some houseboats float on rivers and lakes. Others move on oceans. Some boats travel far!

Inside a Houseboat

A houseboat has a deck. People fish from the deck. They wave at other boats!

deck

The captain moves the boat from the **cockpit**. An **engine** powers the boat.

Parts of a Houseboat

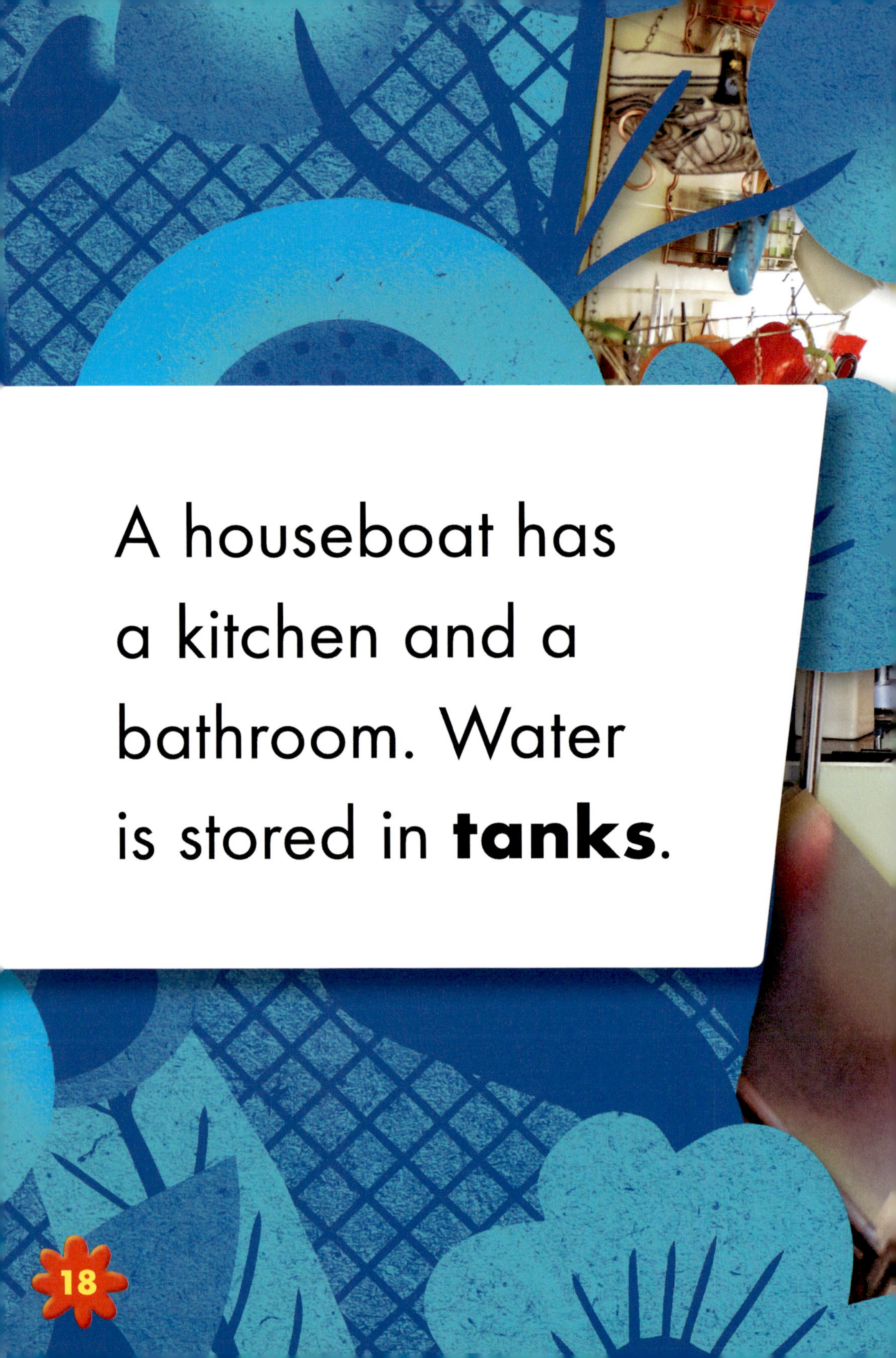

A houseboat has a kitchen and a bathroom. Water is stored in **tanks**.

kitchen
tank

People sleep in **cabins**. Some cabins have bunk beds. These homes are fun places to live!

cabin with
bunk beds

Glossary

cabins

rooms in a houseboat where people can sleep

cockpit

the part of a houseboat where the captain moves the boat

engine

a machine that powers a houseboat

marinas

places where people can park boats

slips

parking spaces for boats in a marina

tanks

large objects that hold water

To Learn More

AT THE LIBRARY

Anthony, William. *Boats*. Minneapolis, Minn.: Jump!, 2024.

Duling, Kaitlyn. *Cruise Ships*. Minneapolis, Minn.: Bellwether Media, 2026.

Rathburn, Betsy. *Vans*. Minneapolis, Minn.: Bellwether Media, 2027.

ON THE WEB

FACTSURFER

Factsurfer.com gives you a safe, fun way to find more information.

1. Go to www.factsurfer.com.
2. Enter "houseboats" into the search box and click 🔍.
3. Select your book cover to see a list of related content.

Index

The images in this book are reproduced through the courtesy of: Dmitry Rukhlenko, front cover; Formatoriginal, p. 3 (steering wheel); Rawpixel.com, p. 3 (wave); Iuliia Sokolovsak, pp. 4-5, 8-9, 12-13, 13 (inset); VEX Collective, pp. 6-7; Pixelmagic, pp. 10-11; demerzel21, p. 11 (slips); Afsha Raahela, pp. 14-15; martinedoucet, p. 15 (inset); lenaivanova2311, pp. 16-17; Pavel Timofeev, p. 17 (parts); Pauws99, p. 17 (engine); JohnnyGreig/ Getty Images, pp. 18-19; South China Morning Post/ Getty Images, p. 19 (tank); Frank and Helena/ Getty Images, pp. 20-21; Abu Sadek Setu, pp. 21 (bunk beds), 22 (cabins); Savany, p. 22 (cockpit); Bobinson K B/ Wikicommons, p. 22 (engine); Artsy, p. 22 (marinas); jesper Sohof, p. 22 (slips); Roman Zaiets, p. 22 (tanks).